The Dhamma Leaf Series

ISBN-13: 978-1499653229, ISBN-10: 1499653220

1st print in June 2014

Dhamma Sukha Meditation Center
8218 County Road 204
Annapolis, MO 63620
U.S.A.

Phone: +1 (573) 546-1214

[wwww.dhammasukha.org]
[info@dhammasukha.org]

Acknowledgements

My thanks to Reverend Sister Khema at the Dhamma Sukha Meditation Center in Missouri who contributed to the main editing on this particular sutta, and who suggested the arrangement as an independent booklet.

Thanks to David Johnson who edited and organized the booklet's content and took care of logistics and publishing.

Sutta translation © Bhikkhu Ñāṇamoli and Bhikkhu Bodhi 1995, 2001. Reprinted from The Middle Length Discourses of the Buddha: A Translation of the Majjhima Nikāya; With permission of Wisdom Publications, 199 Elm Street, Somerville, MA 02144 U.S.A., [wisdompubs.org]

Venerable Bhante Vimalaraṃsi Mahāthera shares the merit of this booklet with all my students, past and present, the editors and collaborators of this book, Bhikkhu Ñāṇamoli and Bhikkhu Bodhi and Wisdom Publications, and with my parents who supported and raised me.

Preface

The Sammādiṭṭhi Sutta
MN-9: Harmonious Perspective (right understanding)

*A sutta which expounds in sixteen ways what "a man of right
understanding" is. There are to be heard in the Buddhist world
confused and vague voices which proclaim that everyone is free to
believe what they like in Buddhism.*

*This amounts to saying that there is no such thing as Right
Understanding in the Buddha's Teachings. But not only in this
sutta but all through the various collections of discourses, one
comes upon formulations of wrong understanding (with the
reasons clearly stated why they are wrong), right understanding
as taught by the Buddha, and anyone else who taught or teaches
in agreement with Dhamma — this last leading on by practice
and attainment to perfect understanding (the Pāli word sammā
can mean either "right" or "perfect").*

*If you wish to reach the perfect under-standing of the arahat, then
it is necessary to know, and to put your knowledge into practice,
what right understanding is. You should know these various
formulations of right understanding so that when you meet
situations in your own life where they apply, you can use them.
You should know them clearly so that if asked: "What is right
understanding about the Four Noble Truths?" you can answer
readily.*

*Of course, the extent to which you can explain any point of
Dhamma will depend not so much upon your learning as upon
your practice. Learning piles up facts, but does not clear mind as*

practice does.

These aspects of right understanding become clear to those who practice moral conduct, meditation, and have grown in insight-wisdom. The more you practice the greater will your understanding be.

Initially though, you should go through these sixteen headings one by one — the profitable and unprofitable, nutriment, the Four Noble Truths, ageing and death, birth (of action), being (habitual tendency), clinging, craving, feeling, contact, the sixfold base, name and form, consciousness, formations, ignorance, distractions, and ask oneself: "Do I know what is right understanding in this case?"

The above was taken from "The treasury of the Dhamma translated by Phra Kantipalo.

The rest of this booklet is a compilation of two talks presented by Venerable Bhante Vimalaraṁsi on 24th August 2005 and 7th July 2007

The 8-Fold Path in Practical Terms by Venerable Bhante Vimalaramsi

This article on the 8-fold path was written in 2005 by Bhante Vimalaramsi and is presented here so it will help you to understand more about its importance when examining this sutta. Coming back and using this as a reference will help you to understand it even better. The sutta and its commentary will follow this immediately.

There are actually many different ways and levels to talk about the 8-Fold Path which is the most important facet of the Buddha's Teachings, when seen in Dependent Origination. The way we need to discuss this is through the applied aspects of doing the meditation and using a much deeper but still a very practical approach to understanding how the 8 fold path works.

The normal ways of thinking about the 8-Fold Path are:

Right View
Right Thought
Right Speech
Right Action
Right Livelihood
Right Effort
Right Mindfulness
Right Concentration

They are commonly put into three categories Wisdom (Pañña), Morality (Sīla) and Concentration or collectedness (Samādhi). But actually all of this is only the surface way of looking at this. The explanation about this path that will be discussed here is a much deeper way that relates directly to one's observations of Dependent Origination and the three characteristics of all existence.

In order to present a little different way of looking at this, things have been changed a bit, so it will become easier to understand. The reason is, when this Path is broken into three categories, the middle category (sīla) is most often forgotten about. This is because morality (sīla) when looked at this way doesn't really seem to have anything to do with one's meditation practice. This kind of dividing up of the 8-Fold Path can effectively change it to a 5-fold Path. This kind of surface interpretation doesn't tend to help or deepen one's own personal investigation and understanding of the Dhamma!

When the changes in both words and meaning are shown and explained it will become clearer. The reason that this is done is because this 8-Fold Path is so important that the Buddha included it in the very first discourse that he gave, The Dhammacakkappattana Sutta (The Turning of the Wheel of Dhamma). He was teaching the first 5 ascetics about the correct way to practice meditation, and was showing how his understanding of the Dhamma was different from other teachings. As it says in many suttas the Dhamma is well expounded by the Buddha, it is immediately effective, has the invitation to come and see,

which leads to final liberation here and now.

What this says is that this Path to the cessation of suffering, is still an experience that can happen for us today, when we practice the oldest known teachings of the Buddha closely. This wonderful Path to the cessation of suffering has 8 folds and they must all be practiced at the same time while you are doing your meditation. So every part of the 8-Fold Path has a practical aspect to it and teaches you about understanding how to let go of the suffering talked about in the Noble Truths.

With that said, let us take a look at the 8-Fold Path in a little different way. For one thing the word Right seems to be a little hard for our purposes of understanding. So the author chooses to use the word "Harmonious", instead of "Right". This tends to put a softer approach to the actual practice of meditation. If you use the word "Right", it automatically brings to mind the opposite which is wrong! This tends to make your mind see things in black or white and nothing in between. The word "harmonious" doesn't seem to do this, it gives a more fluid kind of feeling to all of these different aspects of the 8-fold Path. A question that the truth seeker can ask yourself as you live your life is, "Am I really being in harmony with what is happening in the present moment right now?" This kind of question can help you to remember to stay on the Path that leads to the cessation of all suffering (The 8-Fold Path).They are:

8 Fold Path	
Harmonious Perspective	Right View (Understanding)
Harmonious Imaging	Right Thought
Harmonious Communication	Right Speech
Harmonious Movement	Right Action
Harmonious Life Style	Right Livelihood
Harmonious Practice	Right Effort
Harmonious Observation	Right Mindfulness
Harmonious Collectedness	Right Concentration

 NOTE: I will put the standard way of "Right _____" behind most of these as we go along.

"SAMMA DIṬṬHI" - Harmonious Perspective (Right

Understanding): The reason that this is at the beginning of the 8-Fold Path, is because it sets the tone of the impersonal aspects of the entire Path. This Harmonious Perspective (right understanding) is talking about the perspective of everything that arises as being an impersonal process (anatta) to be observed. When you are out of harmony with the present moment (Dhamma or Truth), you are taking whatever arises personally (atta) and then there is the personal want to control all thoughts and sensations when they arise. This is where the craving begins to arise, and craving always shows itself as being a tightness or tension in both mind and body (please remember that the tightness or tension in one's head is a part of body and needs to be relaxed).

At that time, when you try to make these phenomena be the way you want them to be. Anytime you try to fight or control the Dhamma (Truth) of the present moment, anytime you try to change the Dhamma (Truth) of the present moment, anytime you try to make the Dhamma (Truth) of the present moment be any way other than it actually is, it is the cause of great pain and suffering! This is the "First Noble Truth, Suffering" or being out of harmony with your perspective of the present moment, then you are taking everything that arises as being the part of an "I",

"Me", "Mine" (atta) perspective.

Why does suffering occur? Because of the unharmonious perspective of " 'I want' things to be, the way 'I want' them to be, when 'I want' them this way!" This "I", "Me", "Mine" concept or perspective (atta) is the very problem to be seen, let go of, and relaxed - in all movements or shifts of mind's attention from one thing to another. As you begin to understand that all phenomena (Mentality/Materiality, Nāma-Rūpa) that arise (anicca), are a part of an impersonal (anatta) process to be observed, let go of and relaxed into. Then you will be more able to see the slight tightnesses or tensions (or movement of mind's attention) caused by

taking things personally.

The relaxing talked about when you are doing the breath meditation and the understanding that this same tightness is how you recognize all six kinds of craving (Taṇhā, the craving at each sense door). This is where the very first part of the unharmonious perspective (wrong understanding) or being out of harmony with the true nature of the impersonal perspective in all movements and even vibrations that arise in mind's attention moment-to-moment occurs. When you develop a harmonious perspective (right understanding) you let go of this kind of personal attitude, by seeing through the eyes (Wisdom's eye) of the impersonal nature of everything that arises in the present moment.

When you take anything as being "I", "Me", "Mine" personally, at that time, you are not able to see or understand any of the Noble Truths. Why? Because the craving (I like it...I don't like it... mind) and clinging (the stories that go along with the opinions, concepts, ideas and the false idea of a personal self, papañca) have clouded your perspective. This is the way mind pushes you around and makes you think that every "problem" that arises through your daily life is an emergency and such a big problem that it seems insurmountable.

This deluded mind brings up all kinds of dissatisfaction and even depression. The way modern society works these days is, if you can't see exactly how mind works. You take everything that arises as being "mine" personally and then you suffer a lot because, "I want to control this feeling with 'my' thoughts" and when you find out this approach doesn't work – you have the tendency to take drugs and/or alcohol to get relief from these pains and sufferings. Instead of looking at the deeper aspects of HOW mind's attention occurs and how to change one's perspective from "I am this" (the false personal belief) to "It's only this" (the impersonal observation which is easy to let go of and relax). The first step of the 8-fold path is really the key that unlocks the suffering! That is the deep realization that everything that arises is simply a part of an impersonal process (anatta) which can be seen most clearly through the letting go of craving (by relaxing) and seeing all movements or shifts of mind's attention as being a part of the Dukkha! The rest of this path shows us how to do this, also.

"SAMMA SAṄKAPPA" - Harmonious Imaging (or Right Thought): This is the part of mind that works in images. These images can be thoughts, feelings, or

pictures. **Harmonious Imaging** (right thought) is the consciously taking of an idea or feeling then making it recognizable and easily translated by mind. For example, when a meditator is practicing "Loving-Kindness Meditation" the instructions are to bring up a feeling of happiness, joy, calmness, etc. and feel that image. This is consciously replacing an unwholesome image (wrong thought) such as fear, anxiety, depression, anger, sadness etc. that is currently present. Then you substitute that unwholesome image (wrong thought) with a wholesome image like happiness, joy, calmness, peace, total acceptance or any other uplifting image that you can think of. Now you are purposefully feeling that wholesome, uplifting image.

If you consciously bring up a wholesome thought or image like happiness or joy - you are training yourself to develop **Harmonious Imaging** (Right Thought). In the Majjhima Nikaya Sutta # 19 it says "Whatever one frequently thinks and ponders on, this is the inclination of their mind!"

It is necessary to develop the skill of consciously manifesting a wholesome image of happiness and peace in one form or another so happiness, joy and relief will be present in all of our activities. When you are practicing the breathing and relaxing meditation any distraction that pulls your attention away from the object of meditation, like lust, aversion, restlessness, etc. is considered to be a type of unwholesome image. The letting go of that **unharmonious image** (wrong thought) and relaxing, then redirecting mind's attention back to the breath and relaxing is considered to be developing **Harmonious Imaging** (right thought) with a wholesome object of meditation. Why? Because they are seen and acted on, in an impersonal way (**Harmonious Perspective** – right understanding, Anatta)

On the other hand, if you unconsciously have the image of dissatisfaction, sadness, anxiety, frustration, worry, criticism, pride, fear, or anger etc. you are indulging in

the **Unharmonious Imaging** (wrong thought) which leads to suffering and pain. Being out of harmony with an image that you hold on to causes you to want to control and to fight with what is in the present moment. This pulls you away from the present moment and you begin to think of all of the reasons that you don't like that image. This is how craving and clinging to the false idea of a self or atta identification (unharmonious perspective) arises. These images lead us to lots of suffering and dissatisfaction, in the present moment.

As stated earlier anytime you take an image, of what arises in the present moment to be "I", "Me", "Mine" personally, you will try to control it, fight with it, and force the present moment to be anything other than it is, this is the cause of your pain and dissatisfaction (Dukkha). When you notice this habit of indulging in unharmonious images (wrong thought - feelings, opinions, thoughts, emotions, etc. that are identified with as being mine personally - atta) and you are able to gently relax and let go of that image and then softly replace it with a **harmonious image** (right thought), you are following the path that leads to the cessation of suffering. Again, this can be a way of thinking, feeling or conceptual opinions. Letting go of those things that you take personally, then relaxing and substituting them with an uplifting image leads you to a clear perspective (harmonious perspective) of how mind works – it is being in harmony with the present moment that has no suffering in it. This is how the first two parts of the 8-fold path interact with each other.

"SAMMA VACA" - Harmonious Communication (Right

Speech): This has to do with the gentle communication with yourself (internal dialogue) as well as with other people too. This helps you to easily let go of and relax into any type of disturbing thoughts, feelings, or emotions that can pull mind's attention away from the meditation object (which for practical purposes we can say is the breath, relaxing and smiling or metta, relaxing and smiling). Any kind of self-criticism, or any kind of anger, dislike, worry, anxiety, dissatisfaction, condemnation, or a want to "make things be the way 'I' want them to be" in your communication with yourself (your internal dialogue, for example, anger with yourself, criticism of yourself, dislike of your own actions and thoughts) and others is being out

of harmony (wrong speech) with the present moment.

This leads to a personal belief that all thoughts, opinions and concepts are "I", "Me", "Mine" (atta –Wrong View) and leads to excessive clinging or thinking about. Being out of harmony with your own communications leads you to a hard mind toward yourself and everyone around you. This definitely leads you to being out of harmony with any external communication with other people. The practice of mental development is learning how to lovingly-accept whatever arises in the present moment and communicating this acceptance to yourself and others. Or you could say that one of the things you need to practice is loving the person you are with and speaking with that love. But who do you spend most of your time with? That's right, you spend more time with yourself than you do with any other person, so you really need to practice being loving and kind to yourself, as much as possible. The Buddha said, "Anyone who truly loves themselves will never harm another person". This is why you carry a smile around with you all of the time. So smile and be happy then cultivate those thoughts and communicate this happiness with yourself internally as well as externally to other people! Especially, with the love and acceptance of yourself about yourself.

"SAMMA KAMMANTA" - Harmonious Movement (or

Right Action): This is very important when you are learning how to meditate! Seeing the movements of how mind's attention goes from one thing to another is what meditation is all about! Why? Because when you train your observation powers (right mindfulness) you begin to see clearly exactly how mind's attention goes from being on the breath and relaxing to a sound, sight, taste, smell, touch or thought. This is clearly observing exactly how the movements of mind's attention is seeing the process of Dependent Origination and how it occurs. Being in harmony, is the way of seeing the impersonal nature of all of these slight movements and processes. The more interest you put into watching how mind's attention occurs the more precise your understanding becomes. This observation of how mind's attention works is especially helpful in letting go and relaxing when one has a hindrance or distraction (Nīvaraṇa) arise.

When you don't like or don't see the way mind's attention moves and try to control how this movement occurs then you are experiencing unharmonious movement (or wrong action). For instance, when a hindrance or distraction (Nīvaraṇa) arises like restlessness, when you try to push the hindrance away or to stop the hindrance from being in the present moment, this trying to stop mind's movements is

what we can call **Unharmonious Movement** (Wrong action). Or if you try to stop or suppress mind's natural movements by practicing one-pointed concentration (this includes moment-to-moment concentration – Khanika Samadhi, access concentration – Upacara Samadhi, and full absorption or ecstatic concentration – Appana Samadhi all of these types of concentration are considered to be different forms of one-pointed concentration), the force of that concentration will temporarily stop mind's moving for a short period of time. But when the one-pointed concentration meditator loses their strong concentration, then the movements of mind's attention tends to become

stronger. This is how **unharmonious perspectives** (wrong view), **unharmonious images** (wrong thoughts),

and **unharmonious communications** (wrong speech), in your daily activities arises which can cause huge amounts of suffering and dissatisfaction (Dukkha). This is where true self-responsibility for your own actions can really be seen! Seeing exactly how mind's attention moves from one object to another takes interest, and precision. Watching these slight movements of mind's attention is the thing that makes meditation so incredibly interesting and fun to observe.

"SAMMA ĀJĪVA" - **Harmonious Lifestyle** (or Right

Livelihood): This has always been a curious part of the 8-

Fold Path. The standard way of describing this has been not to kill living beings on purpose, not to sell poisons or weapons, and not to deal in slavery and selling human beings. But how does this relate directly to your meditation practice? If it is important enough to be put in the 8-Fold Path, then there must be more to it that leads to the cessation of suffering. Don't you agree?

These above things do give us this idea of right livelihood (**harmonious lifestyle**) in a general way, but just how

does **harmonious lifestyle** ("right livelihood") relate to your true understanding and practice? An interesting question, isn't it?

And it becomes even more interesting when you consider that the Buddha gave these instructions with the very first discourse that he gave to the Five Ascetics and he was showing them about the direct experience of meditation practice. These ascetics surely did not kill living beings, they didn't sell poisons or weapons, or sell slaves – so what was the Buddha actually talking about when he

mentioned **harmonious lifestyle** (right livelihood)?

When we take a look at mental development through the eyes of **harmonious lifestyle** (right livelihood), it may make a little more sense. For instance, **harmonious lifestyle** (right livelihood) means how we practice our observation (**harmonious observation** (right mindfulness) and meditation of the present moment during all of the times that we are not doing our sitting meditation (in other words our daily activities).

We are practicing being in harmony with a mind that is

alert, calm, joyful and uplifted (**harmonious movement and harmonious communication** or right action and right speech with ourselves -a short note this is why I encourage students to smile whether doing their sitting meditation or their daily activities). The trick is seeing how, when things are not going the "way I want them to" and mind becomes heavy with emotional issues **(unharmonious movement** or wrong action) – how the observation of how minds attention becomes weak and the subtle "I like it, I don't like it" and thinking unwholesome thoughts (craving and clinging – **unharmonious communication** or wrong speech) causes us even more suffering.

In other words, having a **harmonious lifestyle** (right livelihood) means that you learn to carry the meditation (**harmonious observation, harmonious communication, harmonious imaging, harmonious perspective, harmonious practice, harmonious collectedness and harmonious movement** in other words the entire 8-Fold Path) with us all of the time, in our daily activities. In this way, we then truly begin to understand that the impersonal process of Dependent Origination (**harmonious perspective)** is in everything that arises. Having a **harmonious lifestyle** (right livelihood) is having an uplifted happy mind that is smiling, joyful, alert and free from unwholesome thoughts, or feelings.

The emotions that are heavy and tend to pull mind away from the present moment, are the cause of suffering. Why?

Because you tend to take these thoughts and feelings personally, with the wrong perspective of "I am That" attitude. This personal perspective (wrong life style) in our daily lives is the reason that so many people suffer so much! Also, too many times when someone does a meditation retreat, the meditator gets very serious and heavy in mind without really recognizing it. The heavy

distracted **unharmonious lifestyle** (wrong Livelihood) is the mind that is being caught by the personal (atta) belief (**unharmonious perspective**). They become distracted by opinions, concepts, thoughts, daydreaming and the general dissatisfactions of life. Or we can say that whenever mind has heavy emotional states in it, this is considered to

be **unharmonious lifestyle** (wrong livelihood). This is the mind that is out of balance and gravitates toward unhappiness and suffering. When one is practicing

the **harmonious lifestyle** (right livelihood) it makes all meditation and life a continuous flow of happiness that leads us toward the cessation of suffering. In this way, "Meditation is Life, Life is Meditation"!

"SAMMA VĀYĀMA" - Harmonious Practice (Right Effort): Now we come to another aspect of the 8-Fold Path that is quite important. One of the best descriptions of harmonious practice (right effort) is:

When a person recognizes that their mind's attention has become distracted, by a thought, feeling, or sensation - this is the first part of **harmonious practice** (right effort).

Next one lets go of the distraction and relaxes the tightness or tension in both your mind and body, then you smile! The diversion away from your meditation object is a movement of mind's attention toward a distraction (nivāraṇa) and away from your breath and relaxing or metta and relaxing. This is the cause of the tightness or tension (craving) to arise. This happens every time mind's attention gets pulled away and this causes craving (taṇhā), clinging (upādāna) and your habitual tendency (Bhava) to arise. (These are three very important parts of Dependent Origination to be recognized and observed closely) The habitual tendency (bhava) always re-acts in the same way when this sort of distraction arises. The more you see clearly how these different aspects of Dependent Origination occur the easier it is to let them go. This is a part of the way that leads to the cessation of suffering!

The letting go, relaxing, and smiling is the second part of the **harmonious practice** (right effort). The term letting go means that you no longer keep your mind's attention on that distraction, so to be even more precise you can say letting the distraction be there without giving it any more of mind's attention.

Next, you gently redirect mind's smiling attention back to the object of meditation (the Breath and relaxing or Metta and relaxing) - this is the third part of **harmonious practice** (right effort).

Then you stay on the meditation object and smile for as long as you can, naturally, which is the last part of the **harmonious practice** (right effort).

Over the years, I have developed a very effective way of remembering how to do this practice - it is called the "6R's" that is:

To **Recognize** – that mind has become distracted away from the object of meditation;

To **Release** - or let go of, or let distraction be without keeping mind's attention on it;

To **Relax** - the tightness or tension caused by that distraction, this means to let go of the craving caused by that distraction;

To **RE-SMILE** - to bring a light mind that is very alert, and calm to the meditation object;

To **RETURN** - mind's joyful attention back to the meditation object (the breath and relaxing or Metta and relaxing);

To **REPEAT** - the task of staying with the meditation object, relaxing, and smiling. The smile is actually a very good tool to help mind stay uplifted and with the awakening factor of joy in your mind, every movement of mind's attention is seen very quickly and clearly.

That is to:

These words do not have to be said internally to oneself. They are just a reminder to do what each of these words say to do, let go of any distraction that pulls mind's attention away from the object of meditation and it tells how to relax and then come back to the meditation object with a happy mind that has no craving or clinging in it. In other words how to purify your mind of all kind's of troubles, cravings, and fetters.

"SAMMA SATI" – Harmonious Observation (Right

Mindfulness): This part of the 8-Fold Path has been spoken about in very general terms. The definition of mindfulness (sati) has never been very clear! This is one of those words that everyone is supposed to know, but few people actually do. Many teachers today will give the definition of Mindfulness by saying "Just be mindful". Another definition that has been used is to "remember, to remember, to remember", which sounds great but has very little meaning. Now what is all of this supposed to mean? We really need to understand that this important word must have a clear and understandable definition.

The author will attempt to give a working definition that works all of the time in every situation. **Harmonious observation** (right mindfulness) means: "To remember to observe how mind's move from one thing to another". This means to remember to observe HOW mind's attention arises in the present moment, let it be and to see the impersonal nature in all of these phenomena (**harmonious perspective** – right understanding). This is remembering to clearly observe how mind's attention moves (**Harmonious Movement**) from one thing to another, then remembering to let go and let the **Harmonious Practice** (Right Effort) do its work.

"SAMMA SAMĀDHI" – Harmonious Collectedness –

(Right Concentration):

Now we come to the part of the 8-Fold Path that has many different interpretations and many different ideas attached to it. The confusion starts when you take what some of the commentaries say and then place so much emphasis on them. Again, some commentaries are good and very useful and some don't agree so well with the original teachings of the Buddha. The way to know for yourself whether a commentary is good to use or not is by comparing what is said with the suttas (discourses) and vinaya (rules of discipline). If they agree with the suttas and vinaya then you can be reasonably sure that these commentaries are reliable. But when a commentary that divides up the practice into many separate pieces and tends to make things very difficult to understand and practice, then it may be a good idea to let that kind of commentary stay on the book shelf and be used as a reference book, instead of a main book to follow. (note* it is a good idea to use more than one sutta for comparing, in that way when many suttas seem to agree then you can be reasonably sure that this is the Buddha's Teachings)

Here is something very interesting about the words insight and serenity (Vipassanā/Samatha. When you go to the Majjhima Nikāya (The second edition of Bhikkhu Bodhi's translation from Wisdom Publications) and look up in the "index of subjects" the words "insight and serenity" we will see a striking similarity that shows that both of these words are used together, almost ALWAYS!!!

On page 1397 the word "insight" is mentioned and has many suttas to go to for reference, here are a few suttas so you can compare them- 6.3, 32.5, 43.14, 73.18, 77.29, 149.10, 151.19. Then we go to the word "serenity" on page 1404 and these sutta references are 6.3, 32.5, 43.14, 73.18, 77.29, 149.10, 151.19. Do you see the similarities in the numbers of the suttas and even the sections that they are being used in? The point being that serenity and insight are almost always mentioned together and this gives us a clue that they are (as it says in sutta 149.10) yoked together. This means that the Buddha was talking about one type of meditation practice that includes both serenity and insight (Samatha/Vipassana) together, at the same time! Also, this means that the jhāna which is so often mentioned in the suttas, is a very specific type of meditation level. Why? Because the kind of jhāna that the Buddha taught us is a

Samatha/Vipassanā jhāna. It is not to be confused with the ecstatic, or absorption type of one-pointed concentration jhāna, which is mostly being taught today.

The dividing up of "Samatha" and "Vipassanā" into two separate types of meditation tends to make the meditations quite complicated and your progress seems to take a very long time. Which goes against one of the things that describes the brilliance of the Dhamma. That is, the explanation that the Buddha's Teachings are "immediately effective". When you add that one extra step of relaxing and letting go of the craving, your progress in understanding and personality development and your entire attitude toward all life seems to improve greatly and reasonably quickly! In the Dhammapada the Buddha said: "We are the Happy Ones!" and this is what happens when you follow the instruction in meditation precisely and you relax then smile, often.

The importance of practicing Tranquil Wisdom Insight Meditation (TWIM) in exactly the same way as the suttas tells us to do, can't be overstated! Why? Because if you don't add the extra step of relaxing (letting go of craving) your mind and body on the in-breath and relaxing on the out-breath your meditation changes from being a Samatha/Vipassana type of meditation to a one-pointed type of concentration. And because they are not exactly the same practice they tend to have different end results. The one-pointed concentration when used suppresses the hindrances or distractions (Nīvaraṇa) by the force of the concentration (This includes access concentration Upacāra Samadhi, as well as absorption concentration – Appaṇā

Samadhi). The hindrances or distractions (Nīvaraṇa) are where your attachments to a personal self are stored. When you practice one-pointedness concentration and the force of your concentration pushes down a hindrance or distraction, it is not considered to be purifying your mind in the same way as the Buddha taught us to practice. Anything that is suppressed is not let go of, but is stopped from arising while the strong concentration is present. And the suppressed hindrance or distraction has a real tendency to arise, even more strongly, when your one-pointed concentration weakens. With the practice Samatha/Vipassanā or the letting go and then relaxing, over time the hindrance or distraction (Nīvaraṇa) will fade away never to arise again. The Samatha/Vipassanā is the way to actually purify your mind.

The Brahmins during the time of the Buddha and after his death were continually working to change the meditation so it agreed with their philosophies and concepts. They took up using the word Jhana and gave it their own definitions which basically meant one-pointed concentration and they conveniently left out the one step that changes the entire meditation from one-pointed concentration to Serenity/Insight (Samatha/Vipassanā) meditation. Also, they took some of the most popular words and gave them different meanings just to confuse the issues. For example the word "Samadhi" was never used before the time of the Buddha, he made this word up (according the Mr. Rhys-Davies) to describe Samatha/Vipassana meditation which when practiced in the way he describes it in the instructions lead directly to Nibbāna! Of course during the time of the Buddha there were many words in Sanskrit to describe one-pointed concentration and this type of meditation went along very nicely with the Brahmin ways of practice.

This extra step of relaxing when added to your meditation practice is the way to recognize and let go of Craving (Taṇhā). This is why it is so important and is specifically mentioned in so many suttas. When you see that all of the Noble Truths are about letting go of Craving and relaxing of the tightness or tension in your body and mind, it only makes sense to relax or tranquilize often, don't you agree? It does seem to make sense to let go of craving as much as possible because it is the origin of suffering!

When the Buddha came along and chose a different word to use to describe Samatha/Vipassanā (samma samadhi or **harmonious collectedness**), the Brahmins began to use this word "Samadhi" with their own definition of one-pointed absorption concentration which effectively divided the meditation of Samatha/Vipassanā and made it into two separate meditation practices, that is Samatha meditation and Vipassana meditation. Because this was taken to be the way of meditation about 1,000 years after the Buddha's death (in some commentaries) the success in meditation and experiencing Nibbāna began to fade away. Many different schools of thought began to philosophically argue about what was the correct way of practice – but as you know philosophy is the use of words without any action, and this began to change the whole way of looking at the Buddha's Teachings.

With that said, let us take a look at **harmonious collectedness** (right concentration), in the texts it mentions often that this part of the 8-Fold Path is the experiencing at least one if not all of the (Samatha/Vipassana) jhānas. I am going to add the type of jhāna one experiences to each of these jhānas (the word jhana means a level or stage of understanding – not deep concentration). The reason that I include the type of jhāna is so that there is no confusion about just what the Buddha taught as far as the jhāna is concerned.

The first (Samatha/Vipassanā) Jhāna (Level of understanding)

The second (Samatha/Vipassanā) Jhāna (level of understanding)

The third (Samatha/Vipassanā) Jhāna (level of understanding)

The fourth (Samatha/Vipassanā) Jhāna (level of understanding).

The immaterial Jhānas (Arūpa Jhāna) are included in the fourth jhāna as they are different aspects of the deep equanimity found in the fourth jhāna.

Nowhere in the suttas does it say anything about the practice of Upācara Samadhi – Access or Neighborhood Concentration or Moment-to-moment concentration or Khaṇika Samadhi. These are only mentioned in the Theravada commentaries. And don't seem to agree with what the Suttas and vinaya say about the way to attain the full understanding of how dependent Origination or the 4 Noble Truths, or the three characteristics of all existence, actually occurs.

As you can see as we go along the 8-Fold Path these different factors are interwoven and are not separate parts to be taken apart and used. The entire 8-Fold Path works together as an interconnected whole process of seeing understanding and letting go of all personal beliefs in a self (atta). In a way, you could see the different parts of the 8-Fold Path like they were separate pieces of a motor. The motor won't run unless all of these parts are put together correctly. When you use all of the different aspects of the 8-Fold Path, at the same time it is the way of making this Path a good working tool. Separately these parts may work to a limited degree but when they are all incorporated into the 8-Fold Path at the same time it works so well that Nibbāna can arise, even today! The letting go of craving (the weak link in this process, as stated earlier that this is done by relaxing the tightness or tension in mind and body) is the starting point to the cessation of suffering and this Path shows us exactly how to do this. The simple explanation given in the Satipaṭṭhāna Sutta tells us to relax on the in-breath and to relax on the out-breath, **this simple act of relaxing both mind and body is following the entire 8-Fold Path all at exactly the same time** and this is the key to unlocking the door to the deathless.

Every time mind has even the slightest movement in it the craving is the cause of this. Whenever you relax and let go of the tightness caused by this slight movement – you are purifying your mind and this leads directly to the final cessation of all suffering! In other words, the Path that leads to the Cessation of suffering is none other than this very 8-Fold Path when it is used and practiced often!

(The following section is from a talk given on 24th August 2001.)
This sutta has a lot of repetition in it. If you read it out loud or
ask another person to read it to you, you will be letting the
message of this sutta sink into your mind. The old classic way of
having this much repetition in it has very deep and clear
messages that will help your meditation very much.   BV

Samma Ditthi
Sutta #9

BV: The sutta tonight is called Sammādiṭṭi — Harmonious
Perspective (right understanding). The reason that I'm
reading this is because it has the impersonal perspective in
the links of Dependent Origination in it.

**1. THUS HAVE I HEARD. On one occasion the
Blessed One was living at Sāvatthī in Jeta's Grove,
Anāthapiṇḍika's Park. There the venerable
Sāriputta addressed the monks thus: "Friends,
Monks." — "Friend," they replied. The venerable
Sāriputta said this:**

**2. "'One of right understanding, one of right
understanding,' is said, friends. In what way is a
noble disciple one of harmonious perspective (right
understanding), whose understanding is straight,
who has perfect confidence in the Dhamma, and
has arrived at this true Dhamma?"**

"Indeed, friend, we would come from far away to learn from the venerable Sāriputta the meaning of this statement. It would be good if the venerable Sāriputta would explain the meaning of this statement. Having heard it from him, the monks will remember it."

"Then, friends, listen and attend closely to what I shall say."

"Yes, friend," the monks replied. The venerable Sāriputta said this:

This is what they called each other during the time of the Buddha. They didn't have a hierarchy of saying: "Bhante, Reverend Sir", to a senior monk, and Āvuso, or "Friend", to a junior monk. They just all called each other "Friend".

This little simple statement that says, "listen and attend closely to what I shall say" is really a good way of having you settle your mind and let go of any distractions. The closer you listen to this, the deeper your understanding will become. This is real important that you listen with your whole mind, not asking questions right now, just listening to the sutta.

3. "When, friends, a noble disciple understands the unwholesome and the root of the unwholesome, the wholesome and the root of the wholesome, in that way he is one of harmonious perspective (right understanding), whose perspective (understanding) is straight, who has perfect confidence in Dhamma and has arrived at this true Dhamma.

4. "And what, friends, is the unwholesome, what is the root of the unwholesome, what is the wholesome, and what is the root of the wholesome? Killing living beings is unwholesome; taking what

is not given is unwholesome; misconduct in sensual pleasures is unwholesome; false speech is unwholesome; malicious speech is unwholesome; harsh speech is unwholesome; gossip is unwholesome; covetousness is unwholesome; ill-will is unwholesome; wrong view is unwholesome. This is called the unwholesome.

5. "And what is the root of the unwholesome? Greed is a root of the unwholesome; hate is a root of the unwholesome; delusion is a root of the unwholesome. This is called the root of the unwholesome.

Any time you have a distraction or hindrance arise this is when craving begins and craving is the "I" like it or "I" don't like it mind arises. This is the very beginning of the false belief in a personal self (anatta) which is the unwholesome that is talked about here. When greed, hatred, and delusion are mentioned this is another way of describing craving. Greed is the "I" like it mind – Hatred is the "I" don't like it mind – and delusion is the taking things personally or the "I" (anatta).

6. "And what is the wholesome? Abstention from killing living beings is wholesome; abstention from taking what is not given is wholesome; abstention from misconduct in sensual pleasures is wholesome; abstention from false speech is wholesome; abstention from malicious speech is wholesome; abstention from harsh speech is wholesome; abstention from gossip is wholesome; uncovetousness is wholesome; non-ill-will is wholesome; right view is wholesome. This is called the wholesome.

Another way of thinking about right

understanding is seeing and truly understanding the impersonal aspects of all thoughts, feeling, and sensations that arise. This is probably the biggest and most misunderstood thing in Buddhism. The way you truly see this is by letting go and relaxing whatever comes up, in other words, learning to recognize and let go of craving.

7. "And what is the root of the wholesome? Non-greed is a root of the wholesome; non-hate is a root of the wholesome; non-delusion is a root of the wholesome. This is called the root of the wholesome.

8. "When a noble disciple has thus understood the unwholesome and the root of the unwholesome, the wholesome and the root of the wholesome, he entirely abandons the underlying tendency to lust, he abolishes the underlying tendency to aversion, he extirpates the underlying tendency to the view and conceit 'I am,' and by abandoning ignorance and arousing true knowledge he here and now makes and end of suffering. In that way too a noble disciple is one of harmonious perspective (right understanding), whose perspective (understanding) is straight, who has perfect confidence in the Dhamma, and has arrived at this true Dhamma."

9. Saying, "Good, friend," the monks delighted and rejoiced in the venerable Sāriputta's words. Then they asked him a further question: "But, friend, might there be another way in which a noble disciple is one of harmonious perspective (right understanding), whose perspective (understanding) is straight, who has perfect

confidence in the Dhamma and has arrived at this true Dhamma?" — "There is, friends".

10. "When, friends, a noble disciple understands nutriment, the origin of nutriment, the cessation of nutriment, and the way leading to the cessation of nutriment, in that way he is one of harmonious perspective (right understanding), whose perspective (understanding) is straight, who has perfect confidence in the Dhamma and has arrived at this true Dhamma.

11. "And what is nutriment, what is the origin of nutriment, what is the cessation of nutriment, what is the way leading to the cessation of nutriment? There are four kinds of nutriment for the maintenance of beings that already have come to be and for the support of those seeking a new existence. What four? They are: physical food as nutriment, gross or subtle; contact as the second; formations as the third; and consciousness as the fourth. With the arising of craving (tanha) there is the arising of nutriment. With the cessation of craving (tanha) there is the cessation of nutriment. The way leading to the cessation of nutriment is just this Noble Eightfold Path; that is, harmonious perspective (right understanding), harmonious imaging (right thought), harmonious communication (right speech), harmonious movement (right action), harmonious lifestyle (right livelihood), harmonious practice (right effort), harmonious attention (right mindfulness), and harmonious collectedness (right concentration).

12. "When a noble disciple has thus understood

nutriment (ahara), the origin of nutriment (ahara), the cessation of nutriment (ahara), and the way leading to the cessation of nutriment (ahara), he entirely abandons the underlying tendency to greed, he abolishes the underlying tendency to aversion, he extirpates (up roots) the underlying tendency to the view and conceit 'I am,' and by abandoning ignorance and arousing true knowledge he here and now makes an end of suffering. In that way too a noble disciple is one of harmonious perspective (right understand- ing), whose perspective (understanding) is straight, who has perfect confidence in the Dhamma, and has arrived at this true Dhamma."

Lust, hatred and delusion are sometimes called the three poisons, and can also be recognized as another way of saying craving. A good definition of craving is the "I" like it mind (lust), the "I" don't like it mind (hatred), The beginning of taking a false personal belief in the "I", "me", "mine" ideas (delusion).

13. Saying, "Good, friend," the monks delighted and rejoiced in the venerable Sāriputta's words. Then they asked him a further question: "But, friend, might there be another way in which a noble disciple is one of harmonious perspective (right understanding), whose understanding is straight, who has perfect confidence in the Dhamma and has arrived at this true Dhamma?" — "There is, friends".

14. "When, friends, a noble disciple understands suffering (dukkha), the origin of suffering (dukkha), the cessation of suffering (dukkha), and the way leading to the cessation of suffering

(dukkha), in that way he is one of harmonious perspective (right understanding), whose understanding is straight, who has perfect confidence in the Dhamma and has arrived at this true Dhamma.

One thing I want to talk about a little bit is the "cessation of suffering".

The word *Nibbāna* can be mundane, just "every day," or it can be supra-mundane or unworldly. The cessation of suffering: every time you let go, relax, smile, and come back to your object of meditation - that is *Nibbāna*. That is the cessation of suffering. "ni" means no more, "bana" means fire. You're putting out the fire every time you let go of craving and one of these distractions that pulls you away. The analyzing mind, the mind that takes great delight in thinking, is part of restlessness. Even though it might seem pleasurable and real necessary to do, it is a hindrance to your practice because it stops you from seeing what's happening in the present moment, and you get caught in your head. You get caught in thinking and trying to figure out how every little thing works. Why is it like that? We don't care why.

What we want to do with this practice is see how the process works. How does the delight and how does the restlessness arise? What do you do with that as soon as it arises? Because it's a pleasurable feeling, it's real easy to get sucked into it, and think of all the different little ways about this and how it can be used, but that does not lead to the cessation of suffering (dukkha); that leads to more suffering (dukkha).

In Burma, when I would go to a Dhamma talk, Sayadaw U Pandita gave interviews to every one of the foreign monks. There was twenty or twenty-five of us there; Right before the Dhamma talk, he'd just sit back and kind of laugh and talk about, "This really is the "western disease", this analyzing, this trying to figure out how everything works through your thinking. Too bad it doesn't do anything for you." It just causes you to want to do it more, and this is leading to psychological break downs.

The western psychology is about analyzing, it's about figuring out why, but it doesn't lead to the cessation of suffering (dukkha); it leads to the continuation of suffering (dukkha).

We have to let go of trying to analyze how everything works in a particular way. What we want to do is see **how** it arises. What happens first? I'll give you a clue because I haven't done this before there is contact with a sense door, than a feeling arises which is pleasant, painful or neither painful nor pleasant.

That's near to the start of that hindrance, or of all distractions. We all have contact then a feeling that arises, but what happens is — and there's more before that, and you'll get to see that too — but what happens is, that feeling arises and it's either pleasurable or painful.

Then there's some little tiny thoughts, little quiet thoughts, and then that makes that feeling get a little bigger, and the thoughts get a little bigger, and the feeling becomes big and the thoughts become big. Then you're out a thousand miles away, trying to figure out why this is the way it is.

The only way to get to the cessation of suffering (dukkha) when a hindrance arises is to see its true nature, to see HOW it arises. As you become more familiar with the pattern of how it arises, you'll be able to recognize it more quickly.

Some people have come to me and they said, "Well, some hindrance arises because there's a feeling in the head."

There's a feeling before that; you have to look deeper. How do you look deeper? Take more interest in HOW your mind stays on your object of meditation and smile more!

The more interested you are in that, the quicker you'll see mind start to wobble and go away. As you become more familiar with that, you'll be able to let it go and relax and smile right then and your mind will rest on your object of meditation again. It won't turn into this thing that pulls you away and makes your mind think about this and that. So using the acronym D.R.O.P.S.S Don't Resist. Or. Push. Soften, and Smile.

You need to really take more interest in your object of meditation. You'll notice every time your interest starts to wane a little bit and get a little bit weak, all of a sudden you get carried away by one of these distractions, and it's painful. It hurts.

The only way to let go of this suffering is by seeing it the way it truly is. It's not a personal process (atta), it happens because conditions are right. What are those conditions? You're mindfulness gets weak then you lose your attention and do not stay on your object of meditation, and then you get pulled away for a period of time. Then you need to use the 6Rs to come back to your meditation object.

To be able to experience the *Nibbāna*, once you get pulled away, now you got some work ahead of you. You have got to roll up your sleeves and get down to it, you have to be able to let it go, relax, smile, and come back to your meditation object.

What good is all this thinking about anyway? Let it go. Relax the tightness caused by that, and the identification with that, because when you start analyzing, who's analyzing? "I am. I have to find out why this is like this. I have to see all of the different ramifications of this."

That "I" causes a lot of tightness and tension to arise in your body, especially in your head. The only way to get to the cessation of suffering is by letting go and relaxing, and smiling then coming back to your object of meditation. That cessation of suffering might last for just a short period of time before your mind gets pulled away again but never mind.

Every time you let go, relax, smile and come back to your object of meditation there is a little bit of relief. Letting go of the "like of analyzing" is not particularly easy because we've been doing it our whole lives. But it is simple to do when you use the 6Rs.

Our analyzing mind does what we've been taught to do, but then you start to realize, "This doesn't lead anywhere really; it doesn't lead to my happiness; it doesn't lead to the cessation of suffering; it only causes more suffering (dukkha), so I should let it go." Then relax, letting go of that tightness that's caused by the distraction, and then gently smile while re-directing your attention back to your meditation. "No, then I won't be able to think about it more. But the only way I can really understand something, is if I stop thinking about it."

You understand by direct experience not by thinking about it. You understand by letting go of this distraction, as pleasurable as it might be. It's still a distraction and it still causes tension and tightness to arise.

The more you let go of trying to analyze, and figure out why this is working this way, and start delving into your past, and these kind of things to try to bring up examples. All of this is wasted time, you're not meditating at that time. The only time you're meditating is when you recognize that and don't continue, but let it go — even if you're in mid sentence — doesn't matter.

Relax, smile - come back to your object of meditation. Try to see with more interest HOW your mind gets pulled away so you can recognize it more quickly and let go of it more easily.

That is the only way to dig out the roots and the cause of the suffering. Everything else, it might be real exciting, it might be real fun it doesn't lead to true freedom. Open up and let it go, relax, smile, come back to your object of meditation. I wish I had a nickel for every time I said that. I'd be a wealthy monk. It's too simple. You remember I read that thing yesterday where the universe works on simplicity.

We have to get down to our basics, the base of the practice, and that is — as much fun as it is to think — there's pain in thinking. Let it go, relax, smile. Have fun with this! That doesn't mean occasionally there won't be a thought that's an insight, but it happens one time and then it's gone, unless you attach on to it, "Oh, I got to think about this one now!" It doesn't work. We have to let it go. That's where the true freedom is; that's where the cessation of suffering is; that's where *Nibbāna* is.

Let go of all the conditions. Let go of all the little tiny desires and the likes and the wants. Let go of even your aspiration, "I want to be able to get to this or that *jhāna* by the end of the retreat."

All of those things are just more distractions; it's more grist for the mill. The only way we can really progress with the practice is by letting go, opening up to deeper and deeper levels (jhanas), letting go of the slightest little tensions in your shoulders, in your back, in your head, but not spend your whole time doing that, just one time; then smile and come back to your object of meditation.

Over a period of time, all of these tensions and tightnesses will go away, and then there's only pure mind; there's only the pure observing mind. The Buddha called this the "eye of wisdom". Even in the realm of neither-perception-nor-non-perception, you can be attached to things because it is a pleasurable state. All these states of *jhāna* are pleasurable, but the more you like them and the more you want them, the less progress you're going to make in your meditation. That turns into a big mountain that you have to go over, or actually you have to start taking away shovel full by shovel full until it's flat.

The more we can allow, without getting involved in any way, the more open mind becomes, the clearer mind becomes, the more alert your attention is. It's the continual opening and letting go, allowing, relaxing, and smiling then returning your attention to your meditation object - that's your home base.

Always coming back to your meditation object; a strong interest on your meditation; not attached to it, but just real strong interest in HOW everything arises. How it's there, how it disappears, how it's always changing, how it's not yours (atta). It's just there because conditions are right for it to be there. You'll see how fast those conditions change when you start to analyze, when you start to think about. This practice is about continually opening, and relaxing beyond anything you've ever opened and relaxed before, little by little. You'll see your mind goes deeper every time you open, and relax, and let go, smile, and come back to your meditation object.

You will experience the mundane *Nibbāna* many, many times, until finally your mind gets the idea. It does it automatically, and it eventually turn into the supra-mundane state of Nibbana (the unconditioned state). Can that happen in this lifetime? Yes. Can that happen in this retreat? Yes. Can you make it happen? No way, but you can continually keep opening and softening, opening and allowing. You can keep letting all of your little likes and dislikes be, relaxing into that, coming back to your meditation.

One of the more important attributes of the Dhamma is that it is "immediately effective". Every time you relax and allow the craving to go away your mind becomes pure! Why? Because there is no craving and that is the cessation of suffering. Each and every time you realize that craving is the cause of suffering and relax then notice that clarity your meditation is immediately effective and you are following the Dhamma perfectly.

15. "And what is suffering (Dukkha), what is the origin of suffering (samudaya), what is the cessation of suffering (nirodha), what is the way leading to the cessation of suffering (Magga)? Birth is suffering; ageing is suffering; sickness is suffering; death is suffering; sorrow, lamentation, pain, grief, and despair are suffering; not to obtain what one wants is suffering, getting what one does not want; in short, the five aggregates affected by craving and clinging are suffering.

If the aggregates are not affected by craving and clinging, that's not suffering. What is craving? The false belief in a personal self! What's clinging? Analyzing!

16. "And what is the origin of suffering? It is craving, which brings renewal of being, is accompanied by delight and lust, and delights in this and that; that is, craving for sensual pleasures, craving for habitual tendencies (Bhava), and craving for non-being. This is called the origin of suffering.

17. "And what is the cessation of suffering? It is the

remainderless fading away and ceasing, the giving up, relinquishing, letting go, and rejecting of that same craving. This is called the cessation of suffering.

18. "And what is the way leading to the cessation of suffering? It is just this Noble Eightfold Path, that is, harmonious perspective (right understanding), harmonious imaging (right thought), harmonious communication (right speech), harmonious movement (right action), harmonious lifestyle (right livelihood), harmonious practice (right effort), harmonious attention (right mindfulness), and harmonious collectedness (right concentration).

This is called the way leading to the cessation of suffering.

19. "When a noble disciple has thus understood suffering, the origin of suffering, the cessation of suffering, and the way leading to the cessation of suffering he entirely abandons the underlying tendency to greed, he abolishes the underlying tendency to aversion, he extirpates (up-roots) the underlying tendency to the view and conceit 'I am,' and by abandoning ignorance and arousing true knowledge he here and now makes an end of suffering. In that way too a noble disciple is one of harmonious perspective (right understanding), whose perspective (understanding) is straight, who has perfect confidence in the Dhamma and has arrived at this true Dhamma."

An interesting realization is whenever you see greed, hatred and delusion, this is another way of describing craving.

We start to get into the Dependent Origination, and this is real interesting because he only goes from ageing and death backwards to ignorance. What he's saying is harmonious perspective (right understanding) is the cessation of suffering. In other words, harmonious perspective (right

understanding) is letting go of craving, which means craving is the very start of the false idea in a personal self.

20. Saying, "Good, friend," the monks delighted and rejoiced in the venerable Sāriputta's words. Then they asked him a further question: "But, friend, might there be another way in which a noble disciple is one of harmonious perspective (right understanding) whose perspective (understanding) is straight, who has perfect confidence in the Dhamma and has arrived at this true Dhamma?" — "There is, friends".

21. "When, friends, a noble disciple understands ageing and death, the origin of ageing and death, the cessation of ageing and death, and the way leading to the cessation of ageing and death, in that way he is one of harmonious perspective (right understanding) whose perspective (understanding) is straight, who has perfect confidence in the Dhamma and has arrived at this true Dhamma.

22. "And what is ageing and death, what is the origin of ageing and death, what is the cessation of ageing and death, what is the way leading to the cessation of ageing and death? The ageing of beings in the various orders of beings, their old age, brokenness of teeth, grayness of hair, wrinkling of skin, decline of life, weakness of faculties — this is called ageing. The passing of beings out of the various orders of beings, their passing away, dissolution, disappearance, dying, completion of time, dissolution of the aggregates, laying down of the body — this is called death. This ageing and this death are what is called ageing

and death. With the arising of birth there is the arising of ageing and death. With the cessation of birth there is the cessation of ageing and death. The way leading to the cessation of ageing and death is just this Noble Eightfold Path, that is, harmonious perspective (right understanding), harmonious imaging (right thought), harmonious communication (right speech), harmonious movement (right action), harmonious lifestyle (right livelihood), harmonious practice (right effort), harmonious attention (right mindfulness), and harmonious collectedness (right concentration)."

8 Fold Path	
Harmonious Perspective	Right View (Understanding)
Harmonious Imaging	Right Thought
Harmonious Communication	Right Speech
Harmonious Movement	Right Action
Harmonious Life Style	Right Livelihood
Harmonious Practice	Right Effort
Harmonious Observation	Right Mindfulness
Harmonious Collectedness	Right Concentration

23. "When a noble disciple has thus understood ageing and death, the origin of ageing and death, the cessation of ageing and death, and the way leading to the cessation of ageing and death he entirely abandons the underlying tendency to greed, he abolishes the underlying tendency to aversion, he extirpates (up-roots) the underlying

tendency to the view and conceit 'I am,' and by abandoning ignorance and arousing true knowledge he here and now makes an end of suffering. In that way too a noble disciple is one of harmonious perspective (right understanding) whose perspective (understanding) is straight, who has perfect confidence in the Dhamma and has arrived at this true Dhamma."

Moment-to-moment there's birth/death. There's the arising and then there's the passing away. Moment-to-moment everything is in a state of flux, everything is changing. When you see Dependent Origination, you're seeing the Four Noble Truths and the three characteristics of existence in every one of these different links of dependent origin. You're seeing the cause of all of these things, and the cause is the one closest to it. Like ageing and death is generally the last stage of the Dependent Origination, but the cause of ageing and death is birth. If there's no birth, there's no ageing and death. Ok? Also, you see very closely how everything in life is impermanent, unsatisfactory, and impersonal.

24. Saying, "Good, friend," the monks delighted and rejoiced in the venerable Sāriputta's words. Then they asked him a further question: "But, friend, might there be another way in which a noble disciple is one of harmonious perspective (right understanding) whose perspective (understanding) is straight, who has perfect confidence in the Dhamma and has arrived at this true Dhamma?" — "There is, friends".

25. "When, friends, a noble disciple understands birth (of action), the origin of birth, the cessation of birth, and the way leading to the cessation of birth,

in that way he is one of harmonious perspective (right understanding) whose perspective (understanding) is straight, who has perfect confidence in the Dhamma and has arrived at this true Dhamma.

26. "And what is birth, what is the origin of birth, what is the cessation of birth, what is the way leading to the cessation of birth? The birth of beings in the various orders of beings, their coming to birth, precipitation [in a womb], generation (this is describing the birth of action), manifestation of the aggregates, obtaining the bases for contact — this is called birth. With the arising of habitual tendency (Bhava) there is the arising of birth. With the cessation of habitual tendency (Bhava) there is the cessation of birth. The way leading to the cessation of birth is just this Noble Eightfold Path that is, harmonious perspective (right understanding), harmonious imaging (right thought), harmonious communication (right speech), harmonious movement (right action), harmonious lifestyle (right livelihood), harmonious practice (right effort), harmonious attention (right mindfulness), and harmonious collectedness (right concentration).

27. "When a noble disciple has thus understood birth, the origin of birth, the cessation of birth, and the way leading to the cessation of birth he entirely abandons the underlying tendency to greed, he abolishes the underlying tendency to aversion, he extirpates (up-roots) the underlying tendency to the view and conceit 'I am,' and by abandoning

ignorance and arousing true knowledge he here and now makes an end of suffering. In that way too a noble disciple is one of harmonious perspective (right understanding) whose perspective (understanding) is straight, who has perfect confidence in the Dhamma and has arrived at this true Dhamma."

You see if there is no birth (of action), there is no ageing and death. If there is no habitual tendency bhava), there is no birth (of action); and there is no ageing and death. Again when greed or lust, hatred, and the belief in a personal self are mentioned this is another way of describing craving.

28. Saying, "Good, friend," the monks delighted and rejoiced in the venerable Sāriputta's words. Then they asked him a further question: "But, friend, might there be another way in which a noble disciple is one of harmonious understanding (right understanding) whose perspective (understanding) is straight, who has perfect confidence in the Dhamma and has arrived at this true Dhamma?" — "There is, friends".

29. "When, friends, a noble disciple understands habitual tendency (bhava), the origin of habitual tendency (bhava), the cessation of habitual tendency (bhava), and the way leading to the cessation of habitual tendency (bhava), in that way he is one of harmonious understanding (right understanding) whose perspective (understanding) is straight, who has perfect confidence in the Dhamma and has arrived at this true Dhamma.

30. "And what is habitual tendency (bhava), what is the origin of habitual tendency (bhava), what is the cessation of habitual tendency (bhava),

what is the way leading to the cessation of habitual tendency (bhava)? There are these three kinds of habitual tendency (bhava): sense-sphere habitual tendency (bhava), fine-material habitual tendency (bhava), and immaterial habitual tendency (bhava).

This is where our emotional habitual tendency occurs. This is when the habitual emotion of anger, hatred, fear, anxiety, depression, lust, sadness, or whatever the catch of the day happens to be. Many times some teachers will explain the link of Feeling (Vedana) is where emotional states arise but this is not where actual emotion arises. Vedana (feeling) is pleasant, painful or neither painful nor pleasant feeling, it has nothing to do with emotion at that time.

What he's talking about is having a physical body as in the human body or the animal realms. A fine-material realm is the heavenly realms, the Deva-lokas, the Brahmā-lokas, the hell realms, the asura realms, the hungry ghost realms. That's what he's calling habitual tendency (bhava).

One of the causes of habitual tendency (bhava) is your choice at the moment that something arises, whether you indulge in it and have it come back over and over and over again — that is reacting — or you respond by seeing a distraction and opening up and letting it go, relaxing, then smiling. Ok?

With the arising of clinging there is the arising of habitual tendency (bhava). With the cessation of clinging there is the cessation of habitual tendency (bhava). The way leading to the cessation of habitual tendency (bhava) is just this Noble Eightfold Path that is, harmonious perspective (right understanding), harmonious imaging (right thought), harmonious communication (right speech), harmonious movement (right action),

harmonious lifestyle (right livelihood), harmonious practice (right effort), harmonious attention (right mindfulness), and harmonious collectedness (right concentration).

31. "When a noble disciple has thus understood being, the origin of habitual tendency (bhava), the cessation of habitual tendency (bhava), and the way leading to the cessation of habitual tendency (bhava) he entirely abandons the underlying tendency to greed, he abolishes the underlying tendency to aversion, he extirpates (up-roots) the underlying tendency to the view and conceit 'I am,' and by abandoning ignorance and arousing true knowledge he here and now makes an end of suffering (dukkha). In that way too a noble disciple is one of harmonious perspective (right understanding) whose perspective (understanding) is straight, who has perfect confidence in the Dhamma and has arrived at this true Dhamma."

32. Saying, "Good, friend," the monks delighted and rejoiced in the venerable Sāriputta's words. Then they asked him a further question: "But, friend, might there be another way in which a noble disciple is one of harmonious perspective (right understanding) whose perspective (understanding) is straight, who has perfect confidence in the Dhamma and has arrived at this true Dhamma?" — "There is, friends".

33. "When, friends, a noble disciple understands clinging (upadana), the origin of clinging (upadana), the cessation of clinging (upadana), and the way leading to the cessation of clinging

(upadana), in that way he is one of harmonious perspective (right understanding) whose perspective (understanding) is straight, who has perfect confidence in the Dhamma and has arrived at this true Dhamma.

34. "And what is clinging (upadana), what is the origin of clinging (upadana), what is the cessation of clinging (upadana), what is the way leading to the cessation of clinging (upadana)? There are these four kinds of clinging (upadana): clinging to sensual pleasures, clinging to views,

Analyzing, thinking, concepts, opinions, or story about and this is where the big false belief in a personal self becomes strong. Like this is my belief or opinion and "I" am right!

clinging to rules and observances, rites and rituals.

and clinging to a doctrine of self.

This is all "thinking about," all of these different things. Instead of saying clinging, let's change that and read it again. The clinging to a false personal belief means you are taking everything that arises as being "I", "me", "mine".

"There are these four kinds of thinking: thinking of sensual pleasures, thinking of views, thinking about rules and observances, and thinking about the doctrine of self."

With the arising of craving (tanha) there is the arising of clinging (upadana). With the cessation of craving (tanha) there is the cessation of clinging (upadana). The way leading to the cessation of clinging (upadana) is just this Noble Eightfold Path that is, harmonious perspective (right understanding), harmonious imaging (right thought), harmonious communication (right speech), harmonious movement (right action), harmonious lifestyle (right livelihood), harmonious practice (right effort), harmonious attention (right mindfulness), and harmonious collectedness (right concentration).

35. "When a noble disciple has thus understood clinging (upadana), the origin of clinging (upadana), the cessation of clinging (upadana), and the way leading to the cessation of clinging (upadana) he entirely abandons the underlying tendency to greed, he abolishes the underlying tendency to aversion, he extirpates (up-roots) the underlying tendency to the view and conceit 'I am,' and by abandoning ignorance and arousing true knowledge he here and now makes an end of suffering. In that way too a noble disciple is one of harmonious perspective (right understanding) whose perspective (understanding) is straight, who has perfect confidence in the Dhamma and has arrived at this true Dhamma."

If there is no clinging, there is no habitual tendency (bhava). Then you won't become emotional any more - when your mindfulness is strong and you relax which allows the craving to be released. If there is no habitual tendency, there is no birth. If there is no birth, there is no ageing and death.

36. Saying, "Good, friend," the monks delighted and rejoiced in the venerable Sāriputta's words. Then they asked him a further question: "But, friend, might there be another way in which a noble disciple is one of harmonious perspective (right understanding) whose understanding is

straight, who has perfect confidence in the Dhamma and has arrived at this true Dhamma?" — "There is, friends".

37. "When, friends, a noble disciple understands craving, the origin of craving (Tanha), the cessation of craving (tanha), and the way leading to the cessation of craving (tanha), in that way he is one of harmonious perspective (right understanding) whose perspective (understanding) is straight, who has perfect confidence in the Dhamma and has arrived at this true Dhamma.

38. "And what is craving (tanha), what is the origin of craving (tanha), what is the cessation of craving (tanha), what is the way leading to the cessation of craving (tanha)? There are these six classes of craving (tanha): craving (tanha) for forms, craving (tanha) for sounds, craving (tanha) for odors, craving (tanha) for flavors, craving (tanha) for tangibles, craving (tanha) for mind-objects. With the arising of feeling (vedana) there is the arising of craving (tanha). With the cessation of feeling (vedana) there is the cessation of craving (tanha). The way leading to the cessation of craving (tanha) is just this Noble Eightfold Path that is, harmonious perspective (right understanding), harmonious imaging (right thought), harmonious communication (right speech), harmonious movement (right action), harmonious lifestyle (right livelihood), harmonious practice (right effort), harmonious attention (right mindfulness), and harmonious collectedness (right concentration).

39. "When a noble disciple has thus understood craving (tanha), the origin of craving (tanha), the cessation of craving (tanha), and the way leading to the cessation of craving (tanha) he entirely abandons the underlying tendency to greed, he abolishes the underlying tendency to aversion, he extirpates (up-roots) the underlying tendency to the view and conceit 'I am,' and by abandoning ignorance and arousing true knowledge he here and now makes an end of suffering. In that way too a noble disciple is one of harmonious perspective (right under-standing) whose perspective (understanding) is straight, who has perfect confidence in the Dhamma and has arrived at this true Dhamma."

Every time one of the sense doors arises, there's feeling (vedana) that is pleasant feeling, painful feeling, neither painful nor pleasant feeling and then there's craving. What is the craving (tanha)? It manifests as tightness; it manifests as tension in your body and mind; it manifests as the false identification with whatever sense door arises, "This is me". "This is mine". "This is who I am."

You notice it and say something about mind-objects as being one of the sense doors. That means every time there's a feeling (vedana), right after that there's a tension or tightness arising in your mind and body and this is craving (tanha), and then the thinking (upadana) arises.

The only way you can have the cessation of craving (tanha) is by opening up and allowing it to be, and relaxing, letting go of that tightness, that manifestation of craving (tanha). You've heard me say it many times before: when you relax that tightness, you feel open and then your mind takes a little step down and becomes very calm.

There's no thoughts; there's only pure awareness (wisdom's eye), and you bring that pure awareness back to your smile and object of meditation.

This is the major difference between one-pointed concentration and Tranquil Wisdom Insight Meditation (TWIM): One-pointed concentration, you can let go of one of the six sense doors, but immediately you come back to your object of meditation. It doesn't matter whether it's moment-to-moment concentration, access concentration or absorption concentration. You do it in the same way. You bring back this subtle false ego belief (I, me, mine), tightness and craving (tanha) back to your object of meditation.

Because of that one small thing, it will stop everyone from attaining *Nibbāna*, the true *Nibbāna*, the supra-mundane *Nibbāna*. Why? Because when you do not let go of that subtle tightness you are bring craving back to your meditation object and that stops you from going deeper into your understanding of HOW dependent origination actually occurs. Just by relaxing that little subtle tightness, that little tension, and smiling then bring that pure mind back to your object of meditation that opens the way for you to have a completely unattached mind. With that unattached mind, *Nibbāna* can occur, and it can occur at any time once you start getting into the *jhānas*. But that subtle observation is absolutely necessary because that's where the manifestation of "I am that" starts.

That's why, when you have so many different people that might be brilliant meditators, start talking about the ego, and they always talk about, "You got to let it go." They're talking in such general terms, and such gross terms, and people have such a different idea of what ego is.

The false personal belief in a self (atta) is the thing that binds everything together and causes all of the suffering; it manifests as craving (tanha). Opening and letting go, relaxing, not continually opening and relaxing if that tightness doesn't go away. Just one time; you're distracted, let go; relax one time, smile; come back to your object of meditation. Because you weren't able to let it go and relax, you'll bounce back and forth with this until you do let it go by relaxing, and when you do finally let it go then your mind becomes more clear, more bright, and more pure so you go deeper into your meditation.

The practice of loving-kindness is really brilliant because when you're radiating loving-kindness and smiling, and you're staying on the object of meditation with interest, there's no tightness, there's no tensions, there's only the opening up and expanding. But as soon as there's a little bit of disturbance, and that little, sneaky tension and tightness comes up first and then it starts causing all of these other things to arise, now you have to work until you can let it go and relax then get back to this pure state. There's no other way. This is the teaching of the Buddha-Dhamma.

This is why it's such an incredibly brilliant way of mental development; and that's how you start following the Noble Eightfold Path completely, by getting into the *jhānas*. The last factor in the Eightfold Path is always translated as harmonious collectedness (right concentration), it makes me cringe using the word concentration because it's so misunderstood. You are developing a kind of concentration for sure, but it's a Tranquil Wisdom Insight Concentration, it's not one-pointed or absorption concentration.

The thing that makes concentration one-pointed is bringing back that subtle craving and tightness and the personal belief, back to your object of meditation, and then your mind goes very deep, but it also suppresses a big part of your hindrances and personality development. With the Tranquil Wisdom Insight Meditation (TWIM), that opening and relaxing, letting go, there is no suppression of anything. There's only complete loving acceptance and openness, and complete relaxation in your body, in your mind, and with that mind, that pure mind, that's not clouded by any kind of disturbance, that is how you will be able to experience *Nibbāna*, the supra-mundane *Nibbāna*. If you don't have any craving then you won't have any clinging, and if you don't have any clinging then there's no habitual tendency, and without any habitual tendency there's no birth, and without birth (of action) there's no death and old age, sorrow, lamentation, pain, grief or despair. You can see how this is harmonious perspective (right understanding) because you have the Four Noble Truths with each one of these different parts of Dependent Origination, and Dependent Origination is the Four Noble Truths.

On the night that the Buddha became awakened and the next day, he sat going forward only with the links of Dependent Origination, and then he sat going backwards only with the links of Dependent Origination, and then he went forwards and backwards until he understood it very well. This is the thing that when Ānanda came to him one day, he said, "Ah, Dependent Origination, it's so simple, it's so easy to understand." The Buddha scolded him and he said, "This is not easy to understand; this is not simple. It takes a Buddha to come into existence to re-find the subtleness of the way mind and body work. It takes a Buddha mind to be able to see it so clearly, and then be able to explain it to other people, and with that explanation, many people become awakened."

40. Saying, "Good, friend," the monks delighted

and rejoiced in the venerable Sāriputta's words. Then they asked him a further question: "But, friend, might there be another way in which a noble disciple is one of harmonious perspective (right view) whose perspective (understanding) is straight, who has perfect confidence in the Dhamma and has arrived at this true Dhamma?" — "There is, friends".

41. "When, friends, a noble disciple understands feeling (vedana), the origin of feeling (vedana), the cessation of feeling (vedana), and the way leading to the cessation of feeling (vedana), in that way he is one of harmonious perspective (right view) whose view is straight, who has perfect confidence in the Dhamma and has arrived at this true Dhamma.

42. "And what is feeling (vedana), what is the origin of feeling (vedana), what is the cessation of feeling (vedana), what is the way leading to the cessation of feeling (vedana)? There are these six classes of feeling: feeling born of eye-contact, feeling born of ear-contact, feeling born of nose-contact, feeling born of tongue-contact, feeling born of body-contact, feeling born of mind-contact. With the arising of contact there is the arising of feeling. With the cessation of contact there is the cessation of feeling. The way leading to the cessation of feeling is just this Noble Eightfold Path; that is, harmonious perspective (right understanding), harmonious imaging (right thought), harmonious communication (right speech), harmonious movement (right effort), harmonious lifestyle (right livelihood), harmonious

practice (right effort), harmonious attention (right mindfulness), and harmonious collectedness (right concentration).

43. "When a noble disciple has thus understood feeling, the origin of feeling, the cessation of feeling, and the way leading to the cessation of feeling he entirely abandons the underlying tendency to greed, he abolishes the underlying tendency to aversion, he extirpates the underlying tendency to the view and conceit 'I am,' and by abandoning ignorance and arousing true knowledge he here and now makes an end of suffering. In that way too a noble disciple is one of harmonious perspective (right understanding) whose perspective (understanding) is straight, who has perfect confidence in the Dhamma and has arrived at this true Dhamma."

With each one of the sense doors there is a feeling that arises, right after that craving arises; real close. Right after that, right on its heels, is that tightness, and tension that arises in the mind. That's what I've been calling the, "I like it, I don't like it, mind," and right after that there's thinking about all the reasons why you like that or don't like that, and therein lies the analyzing (clinging or upadana) again. We have to let all of that go. You want to be able to have such strong interest on your object of meditation that you can see a feeling start to arise, and when it arises you can let go of it right then, and then there's no tension and there's no tightness. This is starting to give you more and more an idea of the subtleness that I'm trying to show you. This is not any gross state; there is very, very subtle movements of mind, and the more interest you take with your object of meditation, the more clearly you'll be able to see that feeling arise.

When you see that feeling arise, you let go and allow, and your mind will just stay with your object of meditation. There won't be a distraction, and this is how you purify your mind.

Ok, now we get to contact.

44. Saying, "Good, friend," the monks delighted and rejoiced in the venerable Sāriputta's words. Then they asked him a further question: "But, friend, might there be another way in which a noble disciple is one of harmonious perspective (right understanding) whose perspective (understanding) is straight, who has perfect confidence in the Dhamma and has arrived at this true Dhamma?" — "There is, friends".

45. "When, friends, a noble disciple understands contact, the origin of contact, the cessation of contact, and the way leading to the cessation of contact, in that way he is one of harmonious perspective (right understanding) whose perspective (understanding) is straight, who has perfect confidence in the Dhamma and has arrived at this true Dhamma.

46. "And what is contact, what is the origin of contact, what is the cessation of contact, what is the way leading to the cessation of contact? There are these six classes of contact: eye-contact, ear-contact, nose-contact, tongue-contact, body-contact, mind-contact. With the arising of the sixfold base there is the arising of contact. With the cessation of the sixfold base there is the cessation of contact. The way leading to the cessation of contact is just this Noble Eightfold Path that is, harmonious

perspective (right view), harmonious imaging (right thought), harmonious communication (right speech), harmonious movement (right action), harmonious lifestyle (right livelihood), harmonious practice (right effort), harmonious attention (right mindfulness), and harmonious collectedness (right concentration).

47. "When a noble disciple has thus understood contact, the origin of contact, the cessation of contact, and the way leading to the cessation of contact. He here and now makes an end of suffering. In that way too a noble disciple is one of harmonious perspective (right understanding) whose perspective (understanding) is straight, who has perfect confidence in the Dhamma and has arrived at this true Dhamma."

48. Saying, "Good, friend," the monks delighted and rejoiced in the venerable Sāriputta's words.

Then they asked him a further question: "But, friend, might there be another way in which a noble disciple is one of harmonious perspective (right understanding) whose (understanding) is straight, who has perfect confidence in the Dhamma and has arrived at this true Dhamma?" — "There certainly is, friends.

49. "When, friends, a noble disciple understands the sixfold base, the origin of the sixfold base, the cessation of the sixfold base, and the way leading to the cessation of the sixfold base, in that way he is one of harmonious perspective (right understanding) whose perspective (understanding) is straight, who has perfect confidence in the

Dhamma and has arrived at this true Dhamma.

50. "And what is the sixfold base, what is the origin of the sixfold base, what is the cessation of the sixfold base, what is the way leading to the cessation of the sixfold base? There are these six bases: the eye-base, the ear-base, the nose-base, the tongue-base, the body-base, the mind-base. With the arising of mentality-materiality there is the arising of the sixfold base. With the cessation of mentality-materiality there is the cessation of the sixfold base. The way leading to the cessation of the sixfold base is just this Noble Eightfold Path that is, harmonious perspective (right understanding), harmonious imaging (right thought), harmonious communication (right speech), harmonious movement (right action), harmonious lifestyle (right livelihood), harmonious practice (right effort), harmonious attention (right mindfulness), and harmonious collectedness (right concentration).

51. "When a noble disciple has thus understood the sixfold base, the origin of the sixfold base, the cessation of the sixfold base, and the way leading to the cessation of the sixfold base he entirely abandons the underlying tendency to greed, he abolishes the underlying tendency to aversion, he extirpates the underlying tendency to the view and conceit 'I am,' and by abandoning ignorance and arousing true knowledge he here and now makes an end of suffering. In that way too a noble disciple is one of harmonious perspective (right understanding) whose perspective (understanding) is straight, who has perfect confidence in the

Dhamma and has arrived at this true Dhamma."

52. Saying, "Good, friend," the monks delighted and rejoiced in the venerable Sāriputta's words. Then they asked him a further question: "But, friend, might there be another way in which a noble disciple is one of harmonious perspective (right understanding) whose perspective (understanding) is straight, who has perfect confidence in the Dhamma and has arrived at this true Dhamma?" — "There certainly is, friends.

53. "When, friends, a noble disciple understands mentality-materiality,

Mentality-materiality, that is the external object and the sixfold base, together. You understand, "This is a cup." You see that, because your eyes are in good working order. You see color and form, and then perception arises, and you see it as a cup, but at this state, you're just seeing it as color and form

.

(The following section is from a talk given on 7th July 2007.)

"the origin of mentality-materiality, the cessation of mentality-materiality, and the way leading to the cessation of mentality-materiality, in that way he is one of harmonious perspective (right understanding) whose perspective (understanding) is straight, who has perfect confidence in the Dhamma and has arrived at this true Dhamma.

54. "And what is mentality-materiality (nama-rupa), what is the origin of mentality-materiality (nama-rupa), what is the cessation of mentality-materiality (nama-rupa), what is the way leading to the cessation of mentality-materiality (nama-rupa)? Feeling, perception, volition, contact, and attention

— these are called mentality.

Feeling, perception, volition, contact, and attention — these are called mentality (nama). The four great elements and the material form derived from the four great elements — these are called materiality (rupa).

So this mentality and this materiality (nama-rupa) are what is called mentality-materiality. With the arising of consciousness (vin~n~ana) there is the arising of mentality-materiality (nama-rupa). With the cessation of consciousness (vin~n~ana) there is the cessation of mentality-materiality (nama-rupa). The way leading to the cessation of mentality-materiality (nama-rupa) is just this Noble Eightfold Path that is, harmonious perspective (right understanding), harmonious imaging (right thought), harmonious communication (right speech), harmonious movement (right action), harmonious lifestyle (right livelihood), harmonious practice (right effort), harmonious attention (right mindfulness), and harmonious collectedness (right concentration).

55. "When a noble disciple has thus understood mentality-materiality, the origin of mentality-materiality, the cessation of mentality-materiality, and the way leading to the cessation of mentality-materiality he entirely abandons the underlying tendency to greed, he abolishes the underlying tendency to aversion, he extirpates the underlying tendency to the view and conceit 'I am,' and by abandoning ignorance and arousing true

knowledge he here and now makes an end of suffering. In that way too a noble disciple is one of harmonious perspective (right understanding) whose perspective (understanding) is straight, who has perfect confidence in the Dhamma and has arrived at this true Dhamma."

56. Saying, "Good, friend," the monks delighted and rejoiced in the venerable Sāriputta's words. Then they asked him a further question: "But, friend, might there be another way in which a noble disciple is one of harmonious perspective (right understanding) whose perspective (understanding) is straight, who has perfect confidence in the Dhamma and has arrived at this true Dhamma?" — "There certainly is, friends.

57. "When, friends, a noble disciple understands consciousness (vin~n~ana), the origin of consciousness (vin~n~ana), the cessation of consciousness (vin~n~ana), and the way leading to the cessation of consciousness (vin~n~ana), in that way he is one of harmonious perspective (right understanding) whose perspective (understanding) is straight, who has perfect confidence in the Dhamma and has arrived at this true Dhamma.

58. "And what is consciousness, what is the origin of consciousness, what is the cessation of consciousness, what is the way leading to the cessation of consciousness? There are these six classes of consciousness:

You can think of consciousness as potential because unless there's contact, there is no consciousness arising. What they're talking about here, there is the ability for having the eye consciousness, the ear consciousness, and the rest up to arise, but it has to wait until there's contact.

eye-consciousness, ear-consciousness, nose-consciousness, tongue-consciousness, body-consciousness, mind-consciousness. With the arising of formations there is the arising of consciousness. With the cessation of formations there is the cessation of consciousness. The way leading to the cessation of consciousness is just this Noble Eightfold Path that is, harmonious perspective (right understanding), harmonious imaging (right thought), harmonious communication (right speech), harmonious movement (right action), harmonious lifestyle right livelihood), harmonious practice (right effort), harmonious attention (right mindfulness), and harmonious collectedness (right concentration).

59. "When a noble disciple has thus understood consciousness, the origin of consciousness, the cessation of consciousness, and the way leading to the cessation of consciousness he entirely abandons the underlying tendency to greed, he abolishes the underlying tendency to aversion, he extirpates (up-roots) the underlying tendency to the view and conceit 'I am,' and by abandoning ignorance and arousing true knowledge he here and now makes an end of suffering. In that way too a noble disciple is one of harmonious perspective (right understanding) whose perspective (understanding) is straight, who has perfect confidence in the Dhamma and has arrived at this true Dhamma."

60. Saying, "Good, friend," the monks delighted and rejoiced in the venerable Sāriputta's words.

Then they asked him a further question: "But, friend, might there be another way in which a noble disciple is one of harmonious perspective (right understanding) whose perspective (understanding) is straight, who has perfect confidence in the Dhamma and has arrived at this true Dhamma?" — "There certainly is, friends.

61. "When, friends, a noble disciple understands formations, the origin of formations, the cessation of formations, and the way leading to the cessation of formations, in that way he is one of harmonious perspective (right understanding) whose perspective (understanding) is straight, who has perfect confidence in the Dhamma and has arrived at this true Dhamma.

62. "And what is formations (sankhara), what is the origin of formations (sankhara), what is the cessation of formations (sankhara), what is the way leading to the cessation of formations (sankhara)? There are these three kinds of formations: the bodily formation, the verbal formation, the mental formations. With the arising of ignorance (ajjiva) there is the arising of formations (sankhara).

What are the three kinds of formations? Body formation, verbal formation, and mental formation.

There are these three kinds of formations: the bodily formation, the verbal formation, the mental formation. With the arising of ignorance there is the arising of formations. With the cessation of ignorance there is the cessation of formations.

What is ignorance? Not seeing and understanding the Four Noble Truths in each of these links of dependent origination.

The way leading to the cessation of formations is just this Noble Eightfold Path that is, harmonious perspective (right understanding), harmonious imaging, (right thought) harmonious communication (right speech), harmonious movement (right action), harmonious lifestyle (right livelihood), harmonious practice (right effort), harmonious attention (right mindfulness), and harmonious collectedness (right concentration).

63. "When a noble disciple has thus understood formations, the origin of formations, the cessation of formations, and the way leading to the cessation of formations he entirely abandons the underlying tendency to greed, he abolishes the underlying tendency to aversion, he extirpates (up-roots) the underlying tendency to the view and conceit 'I am,' and by abandoning ignorance and arousing true knowledge he here and now makes an end of suffering. In that way too a noble disciple is one of harmonious perspective (right understanding) whose (understanding) is straight, who has perfect confidence in the Dhamma and has arrived at this true Dhamma."

64. Saying, "Good, friend," the monks delighted and rejoiced

They do a lot of delighting and rejoicing in this sutta, don't they?

in the venerable Sāriputta's words. Then they asked him a further question: "But, friend, might there be another way in which a noble disciple is one of harmonious perspective (right understanding) whose perspective (understanding)

71

is straight, who has perfect confidence in the Dhamma and has arrived at this true Dhamma?" — "There is, friends.

65. "When, friends, a noble disciple understands ignorance (ajjiva), the origin of ignorance (ajjiva), the cessation of ignorance (ajjiva), and the way leading to the cessation of ignorance (ajjiva), in that way he is one of harmonious perspective (right understanding) whose perspective (understanding) is straight, who has perfect confidence in the Dhamma and has arrived at this true Dhamma.

66. "And what is ignorance, what is the origin of ignorance, what is the cessation of ignorance, what is the way leading to the cessation of ignorance? Not knowing about suffering, not knowing about the origin of suffering, not knowing about the cessation of suffering, not knowing about the way leading to the cessation of suffering — this is called ignorance. With the arising of the taints there is the arising of ignorance. With the cessation of the taints there is the cessation of ignorance. The way leading to the cessation of ignorance is just this Noble Eightfold Path that is, harmonious perspective (right understanding), harmonious imaging (right thought), harmonious communication (right speech), harmonious movement (right action), harmonious lifestyle (right livelihood), harmonious practice (right effort), harmonious attention (right mindfulness), and harmonious collectedness (right concentration).

67. "When a noble disciple has thus understood ignorance, the origin of ignorance, the cessation of

ignorance, and the way leading to the cessation of ignorance he entirely abandons the underlying tendency to greed, he abolishes the underlying tendency to aversion, he extirpates (uproots) the underlying tendency to the view and conceit 'I am,' and by abandoning ignorance and arousing true knowledge he here and now makes an end of suffering. In that way too a noble disciple is one of harmonious perspective (right understanding) whose perspective (understanding) is straight, who has perfect confidence in the Dhamma and has arrived at this true Dhamma."

68. Saying, "Good, friend," the monks delighted and rejoiced in the venerable Sāriputta's words. Then they asked him a further question: "But, friend, might there be another way in which a noble disciple is one of harmonious perspective (right understanding), whose perspective (understanding) is straight, who has perfect confidence in the Dhamma, and has arrived at this true Dhamma?" — "There is, friends.

69. "When, friends, a noble disciple understands the distractions, the origin of the distractions, the cessation of the distractions, and the way leading to the cessation of the distractions, in that way he is one of harmonious perspective (right understanding), whose perspective (understanding) is straight, who has perfect confidence in the Dhamma, and has arrived at this true Dhamma.

70. "And what are the distractions, what is the origin of the distractions, what is the cessation of the distractions, what is the way leading to the cessation of the distractions? There are these three

distractions: the distraction of sensual desire, the distraction of habitual tendencies, and the distraction of ignorance. With the arising of ignorance there is the arising of the distractions. With the cessation of ignorance there is the cessation of the distractions. The way leading to the cessation of the distractions is just this Noble Eightfold Path that is, harmonious perspective (right understanding), harmonious imaging (right thought), harmonious communication (right speech), harmonious movement,(right action) harmonious lifestyle (right livelihood), harmonious practice (right effort), harmonious attention (right mindfulness), and harmonious collectedness (right concentration).

71. "When a noble disciple has thus understood the distractions, the origin of the distractions, the cessation of the distractions, and the way leading to the cessation of the distractions, he entirely abandons the underlying tendency to lust, he abolishes the underlying tendency to aversion, he extirpates (uproots) the underlying tendency to the view and conceit 'I am,' and by abandoning ignorance and arousing true knowledge he here and now makes an end of suffering. In that way too a noble disciple is one of harmonious (right understanding), whose perspective (understanding) is straight, who has perfect confidence in the Dhamma, and has arrived at this true Dhamma."

This is what the venerable Sāriputta said. The monks were satisfied and delighted in the venerable Sāriputta's words.

That's exactly how the cessation of dukkha and Dependent

Origination works; exactly, precisely, can't get any closer than that. The trick is to be able to see it for yourself, and to understand it because that is the way that you attain *Nibbāna*, through the understanding how this whole process works.

I know there are some people that teach impermanence, suffering, and not-self is the way to attain *Nibbāna*, but you can see one or all of those links without ever seeing the links of Dependent Origination. And when you see Dependent Origination, you always see these links along with these three characteristics of all existence. It's a real interesting phenomena to be able to delve deeper in your practice, can see how the process works and to be able to catch it more and more quickly, and more and more easily, as your mind gets more and more peaceful.

One of the things that happens when we start to talk about *Nibbāna*, that's the big cloud in the sky everybody's reaching for, but you will have the opportunity to attain *Nibbāna*, and that is called "gaining path knowledge (magga n~ana)."

The real personality change doesn't occur until you have fruition knowledge (phala N~ana), and fruition knowledge is seeing the cessation of perception, feeling, and consciousness seeing Dependent Origination arise and pass away again, and then having another experience of *Nibbāna*, and that's called the fruition (phala).

When you talk about the good qualities of the Buddha, Dhamma, and the *Saṅgha*; when you're talking about the kind of individuals that are worthy of gifts and veneration, there are these eight kinds of individuals.

That is, *sotāpanna (magga)* and *sotāpanna* with fruition

(phala), *sakadāgāmī (magga)* and *sakadāgāmī* with fruition (phala), *anāgāmī* (amma) and *anāgāmī* with fruition (phala), *arahat* (magga) and *arahat* with fruition (phala). It might happen fast for you, it might happen slow, it might be a few years before you get to the fruition (phala). There is a sutta that talks about this and the importance of it if you have this attainment you need to keep your precepts very, very closely, you don't go back into the way you used to be or you can lose the attainment.

ST: So, it's not promised?

BV: Not until there's the fruition (phala).

When you jump in the stream and become a sotapanna or stream-enterer (magga) you don't automatically come out the other side. You have to go with the flow and the flow is always seeing Dependent Origination, seeing how it works all the time in all situations, and seeing how everything really, truly is impermanent and impersonal.

Even though you have the attainment of *Nibbāna,* you still have some work to do. One of these days I'll go through the sutta and show you. You go through some slight change at first, yes you do, and when you get it you walk around smiling for awhile and it's really quite an interesting experience. Then as you start getting used to it that's when your work really needs to take off. How fast you get to the fruition (phala) is entirely up to you, and how serious you are with seeing how Dependent Origination works and the realizations that come along with that; they're pretty amazing. But if you say, "Well, I'm just going to go back and get back into my old lifestyle," then you can pretty much kiss off that attainment. I've seen these kind of things happen, I've seen people say, "Well, it doesn't matter whether I break these precepts or not. I've already attained this. It doesn't matter whether I give in to my lust and my hatreds and all of this because I'm already attained." That's a major problem.

Ok, let's share some merit.

-Sharing of Merits-

May suffering ones, be suffering free

And the fear-struck, fearless be.

May the grieving shed all grief,

And may all beings find relief.

May all beings share this merit that we have thus acquired

For the acquisitions of all kinds of happiness

May beings inhabiting space and earth

Devas and Nagas of mighty power share this merit of ours

May they long protect the Buddha's dispensation

Sadhu... Sadhu... Sadhu....

30362252R00046

Made in the USA
Charleston, SC
14 June 2014